MW00718341

Going Forward
Walking Backwards

By
James S. Ware

Bookman Publishing & Marketing
Martinsville, Indiana
www.BookmanMarketing.com

Dedications

This book is dedicated to my wife, Elizabeth Ann Ware, who has hung with me during all these years despite all of my shortcomings.

This book is also dedicated to all the young ministers who feel the call of God in their lives.

Acknowledgment

I want to thank God for His grace, which has allowed me to be in a position, with all of my shortcomings, to be a blessing to someone else.

Preface

I greet you in the highest name of heaven. And without that name, no one can be saved. The name is Jesus Christ.

I started writing this book for the purpose that it might cause someone else to walk in the pathway of righteousness and look upon the foundation that has been laid for their life. I pray that it will be inspirational as well as uplifting.

I realized at an early age everything I liked was bad for me. At the time, I didn't understand that the flesh works against the will of God. If you are pleasing the flesh, you are displeasing God.

Later I often wondered why God gave us evil desires, allowed us to indulge in those desires and called it righteousness. Meaning that He would tell us to look at it, but don't lust after it. He would tell us to taste it, but don't eat it. And it seemed like the things we thought were so devastating for us or were not good to us wound up being the best things for us.

So I realized at an early age that I was going backwards -- that I was doing everything wrong. If you really want to enjoy life, then don't do the things you really enjoy if they are outside of the will of God. That way, you can really enjoy life and live it more abundantly!

Now, I am fifty years old and have learned you really don't live your life to the fullest until you allow your flesh to decrease, and your inner self to increase. You might say, well what are you saying? Are you trying to tell me that I have to do this? Well, let's sit back and let me give you a detailed look at yourself and others around you. You do not have to follow the pathway that has been set before you to travel. Now in traveling this pathway, you will find that you have exits. And having exits in the pathway usually creates problems because you didn't follow the ordained pathway. We have a tendency of looking at others traveling a certain way. When it seems that their way is the best way, then you find yourself reaching out for their way. Once we reach out for their way, we realize that their way is not ordained for us to travel.

When you come into this world, you come for a purpose, a reason. The more you come to your destiny, the closer you come to your death. When you are growing up, you want to rush to get older. Once you get older, you want to be a kid again. That's something you cannot change or turn around.

Chapter 1

The story goes that there was a young boy who didn't ask to come into a situation, but he found himself being in a situation. His grandmother loved him, so much so, she persuaded his mother that she wanted to take him to raise him. The grandmother in turn passed away. However, she had laid a pathway for her grandson before her life came to an end. Her request was not to give that boy back to his mother.

In the process, the young boy was left with a man, who never had children or tried to raise any children. He was stuck with trying to raise this young boy. This young boy learned the things that he liked weren't good for him. He experimented in every area he could experiment in.

As he got older, he had a desire to stay with the lady he came to know as his sister, who had always been in his life. Later on, he came to grips that, yes, she was his biological mother. Then, he couldn't figure out why he was in one place and the other siblings in another one? So, he started making himself visible around his mother's house hoping she would cause him to become a part of her family.

The more he made himself visible, he saw the less he was appreciated. He was there one day when he had grown to the age of twelve or thirteen. He wanted his mom to say something. He knew his mom loved him, how much he didn't know. So, he in turn wanted her to say something good about him. She had said something good about one of her sons and one of her daughters, who had just won a beauty contest. But she said, "I don't know where this other little boy came from."

Well, that was devastating to that little boy because remember the thing he loved the most was usually the thing that hurt him.

He wondered was it really love or what people can get from other people? In other words, if he could get something from his mother, then with his understanding, he could be a part of her life. If he was not able to get anything from her, then why put himself in that predicament? But he decided to go on and try anyway. As fate would have it, every time he tried to get close to her, there was always a rejection. He saw that it really wasn't any use.

At the age of thirteen, his life began to take a downward spiral. He began to go in the opposite direction because he thought there was no such thing as caring, anyway. He often wondered why God created problems and situations in people's lives.

He didn't have the knowledge of God because the only God he had heard about was when he was forced to go to school. He felt school was useless. What was the purpose of going to school? He knew his ABC's. He knew how to count. And anything else he needed, he could learn as time went on.

Later on, he accidentally shot a young man causing great tragedy in his life. But that great tragedy was turned into a positive. The young man he shot was headed on a downward pathway doing all the things to please himself. The young man he shot turned his life around. Although he was now bound to a wheelchair, he refused to be defeated. So he began to seek a trade. He did things to go forward. It seemed as if once again, the thing that should have been a tragedy wound up being a blessing.

As time would have it, the more the young man went the right way, the more the worse things happened. He began to use alcohol and drugs. By the time he turned seventeen, he found a lady he wanted to marry, but he didn't want her to think he only wanted her for her body. So he decided to wait to marry her before he entered into a sexual relationship. But this young lady decided to go with another young man. Then he lost out. This loss was so devastating he thought the best way to deal with it was to run away. The only place he felt he could run away was to go where nobody knew him and start a new life. Of course that was a problem because to go where nobody knows you, you have to have money. He was in a fix again and didn't know what to do.

He opened his can bank and got enough money to go to the nearest big city about 140 miles away. He went to that city and discovered his family had some friends there. He called those friends up, and they were able to direct him to find a room. He felt now he was in the fast lane.

While in the fast lane, he saw people using other people like he had always imagined. But now, he got a first hand view of it. He found a job then felt everything was turning around for him.

Chapter 2

The young man soon met a young lady who he thought would cause him to move forward. He felt she was someone looking for the same thing that he was looking for.

But lo and behold, he found out the same week this young lady made her living by selling herself. He was just another victim. Again, the very thing he thought was moving him forward was causing him to go backwards.

Now he thought, "Although I lost this, and I lost that, I have a job." But at the job he had, he was introduced to a different type of drug. He ended up doing drugs, not able to keep any money. So he ended up stealing food to eat. His survival was to get whatever he could wherever he could. He thought again his life had gone the opposite way.

Someone told him about Job Corp. He signed up for it. He felt like it would give him a fresh start in life to erase all of his rejecting past.

He would begin to start a-fresh. However, they made a mistake. Instead of sending him to an urban center, Job Corp sent him to one full of rejects that had been in prison or reformatory. They sent him to a Conservation Center.

They felt like they were giving him a second chance, so to speak. Even though they sent him to the wrong place, he wanted to make the best of the situation. He said he would make a new start anyway. He discovered the people there felt like society was against them.

While at the Conservation Center, he found himself walking in a pathway that somebody else had laid before him and not the pathway that was designed for him. So, he took up a trade there and tried to better himself.

He then met a young lady who told him he could serve and do better if he came out of his environment and found another place to stay. He also desired to do other things. In the process of coming out, he met other people, and instead of it being a blessing, it became totally the opposite.

So now he's out of Job Corp. Instead of working in the trade he was trained to do, he ended up hustling, selling illegal substances. He found himself doing the wrong thing again. Then he thought that maybe this was what it would take to change his downward spiral of life. But again he was doing the wrong thing.

A customer decided not to pay him for the drugs they received and threatened his life. He thought, well the young lady who he had met had really changed her life style for him. She had taken a rejected vessel and made it a vessel of honor. But since his life was being threatened, she walked away from him. Others walked away from him, too. Not knowing what else to do, he went to a preacher for the first time. The preacher told him to go back home, over three thousand miles away. Now, he couldn't stay on the West Coast because it would cost him his life.

Chapter 3

When coming back from the West Coast, he decided this would be the best thing for him. He found a job very quickly. He thought everything would go well after finding a job. On his job, he met a young lady. He felt good about his life and thought now it would go in a positive direction.

Another young lady was hired, who he started to encourage. The first young lady he met got angry and threatened his life. He thought, maybe, he needed to go back to that other city he had left. In going back to that city, he met a young lady. And in meeting the young lady he thought well maybe this would be a change of life. She would be something that would make a difference in his life.

As fate would have it, she wasn't. Lo and behold this young lady was a very under aged young lady.

And by her being under aged, she wound up getting pregnant deliberately because she wanted an older guy, which was that young man to be in her life. Therefore, she being very young, but saying she was another age, winded up having another baby. So he thought, he didn't know about the baby, but he had found that she was too young.

He decided what he needed to do was to make preparations to leave. When he left, she broke the news to him that she was having his baby. Then she in turn talked to her parents hoping they could come to a peaceful solution. But a peaceful solution wasn't going to happen because she was the baby girl of four male siblings who lived worldly and ungodly lives. They were known for killing other people.

He thought again, he tried to go forward, but it seemed he went backwards.

Her mother felt the proper thing would be for them to go on and get married. Well, he thought, he might as well marry her. Being married, he still was going to do what he wanted to do. Anyway, he married her, not because he loved her, but because he felt it would ease the threat being made on his life.

Then again, he thought he was making a forward move, and it became a disaster because it wasn't a relationship that he wanted. He just did it to save his own life, and it became devastating. The marriage didn't have five good months. From that, he decided since it was not going to be a lifestyle he could live with, he may as well go the opposite way. He began to get this lady and that lady. He even wound up bringing a disease home. They in turn ended up splitting up after numerous times of breaking up.

And again he thought his life would be better, but after the break up it became devastating. He thought certain people would be there for him, but they were nowhere to be found. He was trying to move forward, yet again he was going backwards.

Later, he decided he wanted to see his daughter. When his wife brought the baby to him, he decided he would take advantage of her.

Chapter 4

The young man's son was born from a girl he had a one-night stand with. Even though she was his wife, she was staying with another man. When his estranged wife brought his daughter to him, they had sex, and she became pregnant.

Later, during a trip of bringing his daughter back to him. The wife took sick and had his second baby, which was a boy. He denied him at first, but once he saw him, he couldn't deny him anymore. Because his son was born too early, he only weighed two pounds and a few ounces.

After his son's birth, he wanted to find out about this God that everybody had been talking about. Everybody seemed to say He was a just God. Well, he didn't see any justice in what God was doing. How could He have a baby born with tubes everywhere who had to go on a preemie machine? He couldn't believe that a God, who was all loving, all kind and wanted all men to be saved, would have such a tragedy in his life.

So he talked to that God, remembering Him from his elementary school devotion when he said, "Yes, Jesus loves me, this I know, for the Bible tells me so." He wondered if there was a real God. If this God that he sang to when he was a kid wanted him to serve Him, then he needed Him to do a miracle. And that miracle was to save his son's life. If He would save his son, then he told God he would find out more about Him and serve Him.

His son did get better, and God did deliver him from the machine. Eventually he started breathing on his own. And he said to his wife, "This is God's way of telling us maybe we need to get back together."

She decided to come back and try it again. It was only a few months before she left again because he was running the streets, following this woman and that woman. So she decided to leave and go back home, which was approximately 300 miles away.

The young man felt he needed to start a new life and to get him another woman. Maybe then, he could take care of both of his children because no way could he take care of the little girl and boy and still hold a job. So he began to search for that woman.

In the meantime, a preacher came to him and invited him to church. A young lady also invited him to a church. He began to get so many invitations to churches. He decided to follow the young lady first. This young lady took him to a liberal church. In the midst of it, her goal was to try to find her a husband. And his goal was to just go because he figured if it pleased her, then she would be willing to please him. Remember, he was in search of someone to help him with the children.

Then he met another young lady who was in a cult. She said she couldn't date him unless he went to this cult with her. In the process of going to this cult, he in return heard some good things! He was sitting there one day when this preacher told him, if someone came up to you, you got hurt, and they wanted to give you blood, then you refuse it and go on and be with the Lord. Because he wasn't in the Lord, the fact that they didn't believe in blood trans-fusions just didn't sound right. He decided it was not worth trying to win her to be a part of that.

He thought he just couldn't win for losing. But God had it planned that a preacher on his job would ask him to come to his church. He was tired of running from this preacher to that one. He decided he would go that Sunday to see what it was all about. He told the preacher he didn't have any suits, and he wanted to know if he could be casual. The preacher told him, yes. He went to church that Sunday, and the preacher took a text, "You got what you wanted, but you lost what you had."

While listening to the sermon, he thought this preacher was saying some things he had heard. He then decided within himself God was speaking through this preacher to him because he had gotten what he had asked for, but he had lost his family, self-dignity and own place. His car was repossessed because he was doing everything he thought he was big enough to do without paying bills. At this time in his life, he was at the bottom of the bottom. There was no place else to go. All of a sudden he heard the preacher say, "You got what you wanted, but you lost what you had. But the Lord, Jesus Christ can give you things that you need in your life. And He can turn it around." He decided to surrender himself to this Jesus the preacher was talking about. Before that day, he had contemplated killing himself. He had heard people say, if you kill yourself, you will go to hell. But there is a heaven where you will live after death. Therefore, he was afraid to kill himself, and since he chickened out from killing himself, he said, why not try this way?

The preacher was speaking about King Saul, who had Goliath in his life. Saul wanted Goliath out of his life, but in the midst of Goliath getting out of his life, he lost his throne to David. Saul lost his kingdom, but he got Goliath out of his life.

Since, he could relate to the story, he went up to give his life to Jesus Christ. He thought that after giving his life to Jesus Christ, everything would go forward, and he wouldn't have to worry about walking backwards again. So he surrendered his life that day. The first week was so tremendous! It was like he was a brand new person.

He thought after a couple of weeks went by he would go back to his children's mother to get her to reconcile with him. He went to the city a few hundred miles away and tried to talk to her, but she had a new life with someone else. She told the young man to get out of her life because he would never change.

He said, "I want to be with the children, so we can live as a family again to make up for some of the mistakes and wrong things that I did."

She said, "You can see your children. But as far as you and I being a family again, that will never be. So you might as well go on and live the life that you want, and I am going to live the life that I have because I am happy with who I am with."

Her words were very hurting. He understood because he had not been faithful. He also understood how he had abused and used his wife. He understood the hurt and pain she had towards him. However, he thought coming to the Lord would be a different thing, and he would believe God to deal with her heart.

Chapter 5

As time moved on the young man decided within himself, he needed to dedicate himself to the Lord. He therefore started a schedule. He stopped driving trucks all kinds of hours. He decided he needed to get a job working eight hours, so he could dedicate himself to the Lord. By the way, he had a problem with reading and writing. He never completed high school, therefore, he was not able to read the Bible. He cried out to God wondering why God gave him a mind to serve Him when he wasn't able to read the Bible.

He dedicated himself to try to learn how to read the Bible. He spent only an hour and a half a day watching TV. He ate, prayed and tried to read the Bible the remainder of his time. He did that for months. For the first time in his life, he seemed to be going forward. He said, maybe this was what he was missing, that he just didn't have the Lord in his life. Having the Lord in his life gave him a different point of view in many areas in his life, to cause him to be a new creature in Christ Jesus. As a matter of fact, one of the first Scriptures he learned was II Corinthians 5:17, "*If any man be in Christ Jesus he is a new creature. Old things are passed away. Behold, all things become new.*"

In the new process, he forgot one thing. He had his old sinful nature yet dwelling with him. In dedicating himself to the Lord, the enemy couldn't seem to get him to do anything wrong. But by him being a single man, he began to feel the desire of a mate. Then the enemy appeared to him in a dream. He shook it off and decided within himself that he didn't need a mate.

The following Sunday, he was sitting in church, and his mind began to wander. In front of him, a young lady seemed to have gotten happy in the spirit, and her dress flew up. His eyes fell upon her thighs. He looked and desired her at that moment while sitting in the midst of the church. He was then totally removed from the sanctuary into a secluded place. He felt so bad, he thought his problem was that he needed to pray and fast more. If he could fast and pray, then he could get himself back together. He had to pray and ask God to help him.

He dozed off to sleep two or three more nights following that. As he dozed off to sleep, he dreamed he was in the midst of another situation doing everything he desired to do to this young lady and with this young lady.

Well, when he woke up and realized it was all a dream, it seemed as if he was going down in a hole. As he fell into this hole, it seemed as if he couldn't catch a hold to anything. He thought within himself, he must get help because he was falling so fast. He was going backwards instead of going forward. Although he had Christ as Lord in his life, he found himself falling, slipping back. Therefore, he went to his pastor and told him it had been on him so bad, he didn't know whom else to go to. He had a problem so bad, it had entered into his dreams. And every time he prayed, he prayed God would keep him with a steadfast mind.

The pastor saw his desire, his yearning to do right. The pastor patted him on the shoulders and said, "My brother don't you know the Bible says, 'We must give account to every idle thought.' And if you are thinking wrong, you have already committed the wrong. If you have lust in your heart, you might as well have created the physical act. If you create the physical act and ask God to forgive you, then you can move forward and not backwards." It sounded like a brilliant idea at the time.

He in return thought within himself, maybe that is what I should do. Go ahead and commit the physical act and ask for forgiveness. Then I can move forward.

Chapter 6

As fate would have it, he in turn met another young lady who wanted to entertain him by cooking his meals. And he thought, well I really don't have a real desire, but maybe if I just go in this step, I will be able to get myself together.

As they ate dinner, she told him she had committed fornication and was pregnant. She came to him because she didn't want to have the baby since she was pregnant by another preacher in this church.

She said, if she could have a relationship with someone else, then she would lose the baby and would feel better about it. He in turn told her, it was wrong to have an abortion. She said, she was speaking about them having sex. That way, if it was not of God, she would lose the baby. She felt it in her heart. And as fate would have it, the demonic spirits prevailed.

Two days after having a sexual relationship, she lost the baby. Now, she believed her miscarriage was God's will to rectify the sin she had committed. At the same time, he thought it could not have been so bad because God someway, somehow put His approval upon it. Although he felt bad about having a sexual relationship, he thought, what the pastor had told him was true because it worked out in her favor not to have the baby.

Another reason it had to be right because now he had asked for forgiveness and God had forgiven him. And he thought, maybe he was able to make it another year, or at least without having another relationship.

Consequently, when he thought the miscarriage had helped him, then the enemy began to work that much harder. Not only did she make herself available, others came out of nowhere to make themselves available too for sexual intercourse knowing they were supposed to be people who said they loved God and followed after God's will.

Now, God became a God that they could do as they willed. Even in the midst of this, they condemned certain things. He said other people were going to hell who were doing those things. But he considered what he was doing really wasn't that bad. Of course, the Bible told him any other sin was without the body. When a person commits fornication or adultery, it was with the body.

So if there was going to be some repercussion from that sin, he thought it would just be between him and God and no one else. Again, he thought he was going forward. And again, he took a backwards step.

Chapter 7

The young man discovered instead of being that man of God he wanted to be, the devil was giving him something he never could get before he came to Christ - women. Because he was trying to move forward in Christ, the devil made sure the thing he could never have, he could have it. He found it was so easy to commit fornication because he had many of the young ladies in the church wanting to commit fornication with him. Not only that, but people who proclaimed to be sold out to the Lord in the church house were totally different after church. And it became a common thing among his associates for them to do wrong.

In other words, everybody, so to speak, was doing it as if nobody was perfect. We all have something to fault whether it be fornication or lying or anything of that nature. He realized he was going backwards in the name of the Lord. And everything he thought he would accomplish, again, it was going totally the opposite way.

In the midst of this, he felt he needed to go forward and begin to answer the call in his life. He thought, well maybe his problem was not doing all God wanted him to do. He decided if he did all he should do for the Lord, that would slow things down in his life or make a turn about.

So, he began preaching the Gospel and studying the Bible simply to get a message for others, never looking at himself. He studied the Bible in order that he might be a help to someone else. But the more he tried to help others, the deeper he began to sink and go backwards in the direction he was going. Because now that he had become a minister, it was not something he decided, but it was a call of God over his life. He felt his call was why he couldn't overcome the snare that was in his life. He felt if he answered the call, this would give him victory. But instead of getting victory, he felt himself sinking deeper and deeper, going the wrong way.

Because he studied the Bible constantly to give a message so when his time came on the 5th Sunday, his pastor would allow him to preach the evening service. He wanted to be prepared to bring a message. All his studying was geared around that. As he began to study, the enemy came more to entice him. He found himself in a position to just about have anyone who was in the church who was single. As a matter of fact, even when he would see someone in the streets, he felt someone was going to say, he was not a man of God.

He began to seek and ask God if he could find a wife. That would cure his lust spirit and cause him to go forth, be a man of God and seek out God's true will in his life, more than just preaching the gospel. He would know the direction God was leading and guiding him to go in.

Well, in the process, the things he had accumulated, he began to lose. Then all of a sudden, he thought, "Lord if only you would do me this favor. Lord this is the problem." He constantly blamed God for not giving him a family. So as fate would have it, he visited a church, and he heard a young lady singing in the choir. For some apparent reason, her voice stood out. He began to believe whoever was singing the song needed to be his wife. And this was the wife God had called and chose for him. She would be a help in the ministry. She would not only cause him to go forth in the ministry but take away the spirit of lust that had gripped his mind and caused him to bring an open shame to the name of Jesus Christ.

As he listened, he began to search out the voice. Suddenly, that voice stood up, and he saw this young lady. It seemed as though she was more beautiful than any other woman he had been fooling with. Every strand of her hair was in perfect place. He said within himself, "I'm not able to talk to that girl. I don't even come up to the qualifications of communicating with her."

When church turned out, he wanted to go and introduce himself. However, he was so afraid to even say anything to her because he felt he was not in her league. Coincidentally, the mother of that particular church needed a ride home and asked him if he would take her home. Of course, him being a gentleman and man of God did anything for anybody who asked him to do righteousness. He said, "Yes."

To his delight, the young lady he liked needed a ride home as well. Her friend, who usually dropped her off, was not able to pick her up, so she needed a ride home. He thought, this had to be a move and a hand of God. But the problem was, he had the old lady in the car. He thought, he would take the old lady home first, then take the young lady home, so he could have an opportunity to communicate with her and try to see if he could talk to her.

After letting the old lady out, he talked to the

young lady. She happened to have a small baby, who was almost two years old. He told her how pretty and neat the baby was dressed and how neat she looked. He then asked her if she was engaged or married. She said, "No." After which, he asked her if she was planning on marrying the baby's father? Again she said, "No." He asked her why? She said, "He was too jealous. She didn't want to live her life like that." He told her that a beautiful young lady such as herself, the man couldn't help from being jealous.

On the way home, she stopped to get some chicken to eat. Since she couldn't carry the chicken and the baby in the house, he carried the baby while she carried the chicken. Inside he met her mother and brother, who were sitting in the living room.

He was so shy, the only way he could ask her for her telephone number was to ask the brother to come to church. He thought maybe she would answer the phone when he called. By getting her number, he would be able to talk to her, or to the brother to find out more about her. In the process, she wrote the number down for him because he didn't have a pen. Instead of her writing the brother's name, she wrote her name. She figured this was a way for him to get to know her. She felt he wouldn't forget her, but he might forget the brother.

As the young man left, he never noticed that she wrote her name. Shortly afterwards, he went to work on a third shift job. When he went into his pocket for some money to get some coffee, he pulled the number out of his pocket thinking he was pulling a dollar out. But he saw she had written her name and number on the paper.

He woke straight up. He couldn't wait to get home that morning to call her to be able to communicate with her since she wrote her number down. Well, he called her not knowing she didn't stay with her mother. She didn't tell him. As a matter of fact, she was shacking next door with her baby's daddy, who she said she wasn't going to marry. Her mother in turn said, "I'll have her call you." And he left his number. Shortly afterwards, around ten that morning, she called. He had just dozed off to go to sleep after reading his Bible and praying. He immediately woke up to talk to her. They had a pleasant conversation, but she still didn't tell him she was staying with another man.

Regardless of her situation, he wanted to talk to her. Luckily, his shyness was not as bad over the phone as it was in person. As he began to talk to her, he told her how beautiful she was, and how he desired someone in his life like her. Pretty soon, she began to think about how pleasant he was. She thought she needed to have someone like him in her life. But she had a problem.

After a few days of conversations, she confessed she still had her daughter's father in her life, and he was very jealous. He would cause great problems. She said, she would try to get him out of her life, but she needed time. She never said she was staying with him. After a week and a half, maybe two weeks of talking to her on the phone, he made a date to take her to learn how to drive. He did that just to get with her anyway he could.

Because he wanted to teach her how to drive, he really thought he was going forward in his life. He began to talk to the Lord about it. He said, "God, I know I haven't done all I should have done as a minister and as a believer, but saying that I love You. I have brought an open shame as a minister of the gospel. But God, if you could just fix it so this woman could fall in love with me. If I could have her, I wouldn't want any other woman in my life. I will love her until the very end."

As he talked to her the third week, she decided to drive. He noticed when she got in the car, she sank down in the seat as they drove off from her mother's house. She then started driving once they reached his designated spot.

Then he said, "Wait a minute, you are driving

too fast!" He reached and grabbed her leg with his hand.

Then all of a sudden, she smiled and said, "You are just doing that deliberately." She said, "By the way, where do you live?"

He told her where he lived. Then she said, "Let me see your apartment." He took her to his apartment for her to see.

She said, "Oh, this is a nice apartment." And she went into the kitchen and said, "This is why you are so little. You are not eating the proper foods. You need someone in your life to cook for you."

He said, "Maybe I'll be blessed enough to get a wife. I eat, but I just don't gain weight."

She in turn went through the house. She went to the bedroom, and she said, "You sure do have a hard bed."

He said, "It's better for your back."

Then she said, "Let me get out of here. I don't want to give you any ideas." Then she walked into the living room, and looked at his collection of records. She looked at the old Temptation records and found he had just bought a new record by

Thelma Houston - Don't Leave Me This Way. She put the record on and asked what he was doing with this record as a minister of the gospel?

He told her, "Well, I am a minister, but I am still a person. I still am a man, and I still have feelings."

She said, "Oh, really!"

And he walked towards her just to bluff her, but she didn't move.

She said, "You don't want to do that. You might get yourself in trouble that you're not able to get out of."

He in turn said, "I would like to get in trouble." So he walked towards her again and kissed her. And from that kiss he told her he was like Thelma Houston's record. Don't leave him this way.

So, she smiled and said, "What do you expect me to do?"

He said, "It's not what I expect you to do, but it's what you would like to do."

He held and caressed her. The next thing, they were in the bed. And he thought, he had done wrong again. He asked the Lord for this person to be in his life. But now, he had gone against the morals God had ordained. Then he thought, well God would forgive us for all sins, so he did as usual and repented. He took her back home when it was over.

The next day, he called her on the phone, and her oldest sister came in the house and said, "I don't know who she is talking to, but whoever he is, she is really into that person. She has slid all the way down into the chair."

Well, someone might not think that was anything, but because she was so afraid of the guy she was with, she felt she had to tell him if she was talking to someone. If she didn't, he would find out and jump on her. He also had fear in her that she couldn't wear certain clothes.

Then she told him on that day she was still staying with her baby's father.

He told her, "How could you say you have feelings for me and love me when you are still with another man? So, I'm giving you a week to get out of there."

She said, "Don't do that. Give me more time."

He said, "You don't need anymore time. If you love me, you will leave him."

She said, "I need more time because you don't know him."

Well, she was facing a decision. Again, he thought he was going forward in life because he felt she cared about him, and he wanted her to make the move. She in turn moved from the man to her mother's. She used the excuse she wore a blouse she knew he didn't like. It was a sleeveless blouse with her arms out. He hit her and told her to go put on clothes. She used that excuse to move and leave him.

She told the young man she had left her baby's daddy. They went out that night to celebrate her leaving him and shortly afterwards he brought her back. The next day, they made preparations to go to church.

Her baby's daddy found out she didn't leave him because he hit her, but because there was another man in her life or was trying to come in her life. He thought within himself, he would rather kill her than see her with someone else. So, he kept the baby. That Sunday before she went to church, she asked him to bring the baby, so she could take her to church.

The young man was going to pick her up for church, but the Lord wouldn't have him to be in the midst of it. So another gentleman, Reverend B., decided he was going to pick her up since he was going that way. But right before Reverend B. arrived, the daddy brought the baby to the mother's house. As she reached for the baby, he shot her with a gun.

She ran into her mother's house. The baby's daddy followed her inside. He found her in the back room, in a corner. He shot her with the rest of the bullets, then grabbed her by the neck while shooting her in her stomach. He emptied the gun and ran out of her mother's house leaving her for dead. Her mother cried and ask God to save her daughter's life.

In the midst of it, she laid on the floor as white death foam came out of her mouth. Her mother began to rebuke death. She said, "Lord don't allow my daughter to die."

When he heard the news, he in turn said, "God don't let her die." And the men left and rushed her to the hospital. She eventually passed out and was unconscious. She went through surgery at the hospital. Everyone prayed.

He made a commitment. "God bring her out of this. Please don't allow her to die because no one else knew I had put pressure on her to move."
He felt really bad. She was in surgery five to

seven hours with no one knowing anything.

Shortly afterwards, the doctors said, "She would be pulling through although the main artery was shot. She had so many holes in her intestines it would just be in the hands of God."

In the midst of it, he prayed with her as they brought her down from intensive care. He believed God for her healing. Then the news came down that she was recovering. She was coming back through.

It took a while, but God delivered her. She was able to come back to herself, and he knew it was for him to marry her.

The word was out, and her assailant still hadn't gotten locked up. He went and paid a lawyer who signed his bond because it was a Black-on-Black crime. The lawyer said this was a just, passion move. He was not a violent man. He was a hard working man. So they let him out. He also said he had a bullet with the man's name on it who she was going with.

His words put fear in the young preacher's heart. He started carrying a gun under his car seat. He wasn't relying on God anymore. He was trying to protect himself. Shortly after that, she was released from the hospital, and the baby's daddy saw her riding to the store with the preacher. He cut them off, which made the car move, and the gun moved from its place. He reached for the gun, but it was gone.

The daddy came to the car and said, "I ought to blow your brains out!"

The preacher told him to do whatever he was going to do. He was afraid, but he was trusting, even at that time, in the Lord.

He in turn said, "You are not even worthy of the bullet."

That was one time he was glad he wasn't worthy of the bullet. So now, she was out and recovering. They made preparations to get married because he had promised God he was going to marry her. But as she became free, she looked at life with a different point of view. Although she wanted the preacher in her life, she wanted to experience some things she had not experienced because she had been in a cage. So again, when he thought he was going forward, lo and behold, he began to go backwards.

She began to go out and party. He tried to uphold his stand as a minister. He tried to find her as she stayed out until three or four o'clock in the morning. He rode the streets wondering where she was. Some nights, she even stayed out all night long. But yet, he still believed this was the wife God had given him.

In the midst of all that was going on, he refused to look at her hanging out all night long. To top it all off, finally the man had to go to court who shot her. They gave him some halfway house time, not real prison time. He only spent a few months in prison. When there was an opening in the halfway house, he was sent there.

She went to see him at the halfway house. In the midst of that, she got pregnant, which was devastating to her. But at the same time, she continued to have sex with the preacher. Now she thought, I don't love the preacher, but I need someone like him in my life because he's nice. Even though she didn't love the preacher, she realized she needed to marry him.

The preacher believed he was going forward. He hoped God would change the situation, knowing she got high, smoked, cursed and did all the things she didn't do before. Because he was in lust and going against the will of God, trying to go forward, he was steady going backwards.

So, he in turn said, "I will marry her."

Chapter 8

On one hand, he really wanted to marry her, but on the other hand, he didn't want to marry her because she was partying and staying out. Some nights she stayed out all night. Even during the week, she stayed out until three or four o'clock in the morning. But the problem was because he was confessing to know the Lord, and he was a minister in the Baptist Church.

He was in a position that he had to make a decision. Either he needed to leave her alone, or he needed to go on and marry her. What really brought it to a head was when a young girl, 4-6 years old at the most, used profanity. He told the girl she should be ashamed of herself, and God didn't like what she was doing. And if she kept it up, he was going to tell her mother.

The little kid told the preacher, "You can't tell me what to do, you are going with A.L.."

As a minister, he tried to do things undercover, so he didn't let everybody see him with A.L.. He thought very few people knew they were actually going together. But to hear this young child say that pricked his heart. He thought then, he needed to get married or leave her alone. He came home and told her they were going to marry, and he married her shortly thereafter.

Once they got married, for the first month, it seemed like he made the right decision. But as fate would have it, she became restless because she couldn't do the things she was doing. Soon she took all she could take, and she started going back out. One particular time she went out, she came home with a scarf tied around her neck.

He had a third shift job at the time. She thought he saw her, but he didn't because he got home around seven-thirty that morning and didn't see her come in the door. But he saw the passion marks on her neck. She said because she wouldn't go to bed with this guy, he decided to put passion marks on her neck, so her husband would know she had been out with another man. That was the excuse she told him. Well, because things were getting so difficult, he didn't believe it, and the thing hurt him badly. He thought the reason he was having that problem was because he was disobedient to God. He knew the Scriptures had said, "*How can two walk together, except they agree?*"

He thought in order to go forward in his life, he needed to repent and be obedient to what God had told him about going to another city. But, he was so concerned about being with this woman, he refused to be obedient. Finally, he decided now he must do what he needed to do. He went to a large city in the South where he found a job with Nabisco Cookie Company.

He thought getting the job had to be the sign he was being obedient to God. He found the job when he wasn't really looking for one because he was lost at the time he got the job. By him finding this job, the guy talked to him about Jesus Christ.

He said, "I don't take applications on Monday, but since you are a special person, I will process it." Before he could get back home from that city, the guy had called him and said he had a job.

Now he thought, the new job was his way out of his marriage. He was going to ask her to come to the city. Since she had never left home, he felt she was not going to come.

In the meantime, he would commute back and forth for a little while. He thought commuting would get old, and they would go their separate ways. After being gone for a month, she decided she needed to get a job to help out while he got established. While at work, she hurt her finger in a machine. He immediately rushed home and realized he didn't want to leave her as badly as he thought he did. So he asked her to come to the large city in the South.

She said, "I don't want to go." Then she thought, "If I can party here, then I can really party there." Because she had heard so much about that city, she said she would come.

He moved their furniture and found a little apartment in the city. Here again, he thought he was doing good and everything was going to be better because he knew she didn't know too many people there. He wouldn't have to worry about her going out with guys and doing the things she was doing in the city that they were from. But her motive was to do even greater things than what she was doing at home.

Consequently, he became a baby sitter. Now he had her child, and the child she got pregnant with after they got together. One night she came home between four or five in the morning. And she told him about a Caucasian man who asked her to dance on the table.

The White man said, "You in the black and white dress. Why won't you dance for me?"

It pricked the young man's heart so bad, he laid wondering where she was and what she was doing. When she came home, he jumped in the bed and acted as though he was asleep. But he had been up pacing the floor wondering who she was with and where she was? One particular time when she said he seemed different, it was because his heart was pierced. She had hurt him when she came home after being out all night with the baby in one seat, and she was in another seat according to her.

He reached a point where he had to make a decision. He went to the bathroom and said, "Lord, either save her or get her out of my life. I have come to the end of my rope. I know I made a mistake, and I know I did those things I truly should not have done. I committed fornication. I not only committed fornication, I chose an unsaved mate. But right now God, if you are truly the God of my life, I want you to bring forth a change in my household."

After he prayed, he was looking for the Lord to let some man come into her life to leave him, so he would have an excuse to start his life all over again.

He was hoping something happened to get her out of his life. But as fate would have it, the Lord chose two weeks from that to save her in a little church right up from the house. She decided she wanted to go to this church, and in going there, she was saved.

Well, he thought it was going to be good then. He felt he was really going forward the first time in his life. He had gotten himself in a good position. He had a saved wife. He would forgive her for anything she had done in the past. He would move forward.

Although he thought they were going forward, she had a different point of view. She got with a group of people who felt like no one was right but their group. So now, they had a great division. She began to say, "Jesus, Jesus, Jesus" every time anyone talked to her. The moment anyone tried to talk back, she considered them as the enemy and would say, "Jesus, Jesus, Jesus" to drive the so-called demon away from her. It got so bad, she didn't want to have any part of anything he suggested. So, the very time he thought he was going forward, he was going backwards. It was so bad because at first she was a sinner, and they were going along a different pathway. Now, they were enemies not able to communicate, which made their relationship even more devastating.

Chapter 9

He thought there was no relief, so he began to look for a relief in people. He found himself complaining. As he complained about the situation, he found that people gave him special attention. Because he had an inferiority complex about himself while growing up, he decided attention was truly what he needed. As time went on, he continued to complain, and people listened. She became a villain, and he became a saint.

Shortly thereafter, he started running into young ladies who he complained to, and they really wanted to come into his life. They felt if she was doing all of that, then he needed to leave her.

He felt he needed to be with somebody who really cared for him. He met a young lady with the initials of C.D.. Miss C.D. was a young lady who a friend of his liked. But she didn't like the friend. So, the friend thought if he got the preacher to talk to her, then that would help the friend out. He thought if he could talk to her for the friend, then he could tell her how much she could be a part of the friend's life.

Well, in the process, they became good friends. She told him, she was not interested in a relationship with his friend. She wound up being his so-called crying partner. Again, he thought he was going forward. Now he had someone to listen to him. She was nice. She was not concerned about going with him because she was in love with someone else. So, he didn't have to worry about her looking at him in a different way.

However, to their surprise, the guy she was looking to marry, he was already married. She was so hurt to find out a month before she was to marry that her fiancé was already married, she went back home to a small town.

He convinced C.D. she should come back to the big city to find a job and get on her feet. At this time, he had found a good job at one of the well-known Teamster Union Companies. He could help her.

With him convincing her to return, she eventually came back to her sister's house. Her sister asked him to come over there to see her sister, who was hiding in the back room. When she came out, they hugged as a greeting. He felt like it was different. For that reason, they started doing things together such as going out to eat, having breakfast, and having lunch. Because she always encouraged him, he never suspected their friendship would get out of hand. Even though he started fighting back feelings he had developed for her.

Although he cared for C.D, he had no excuse to do wrong. His wife now confessed to know the Lord. Also, she never denied him of her body in time of sexual need unless she was sick or something.

Soon his wife's eyes became open to the cult group she was with because she began to remember how he stayed steadfast when she blew money or smoked in his face. She believed if anyone was saved, it was her husband. He had to be saved to put up with some of the things she put him through. For that reason, she came away from her church to be as a family with him.

Now he didn't have anything to complain about. And C.D. would say, "After all, that's your wife" when he talked about his wife to her. It made him feel good his wife was not trying to do anything out of the ordinary. But now, he found himself fighting back feelings for C.D..

For the first time, his wife sought God and asked Him to give her love for the man she had married. She had an unconditional love. She loved him regardless of what he did or said. At this time, however, all his attention was headed towards C.D..

When he was in Florida with C.D., the enemy had a man from Florida to be in the restroom with him. As they moved toward washing their hands, this man said to him, "You don't know me do you?"

And he said, "No."

He said, "But because you spoke and said praise the Lord. How you doing? I want you to know God has a message for you. The woman you are married to is not the wife God wanted you to have. The woman He really wanted you to have is the woman you like. And if you would admit it, you're in love with her."

Now, he was devastated. This man didn't know him from nobody, but he knew it wasn't a setup in anyway. But Satan himself conjured it up. However, at the time, he wasn't able to see that.

Before the man departed, he got his address and told him he was going to pray on it and let him know

what's what within the near future. And he appreciated him being obedient to God. He came home and
tried to find a problem because he needed an excuse
to leave home. But he didn't know how he could
leave home without knowing this woman was truly
his. So, he prayed and asked God because he didn't
want to go forward again and find himself going
backwards. Then he thought the best thing to do was
to lay his cards on the table with C.D., to let her
know, for the first time, he was in love with her. He
wanted her to be in his life.

He took her out to eat at a Mexican restaurant to
break the news to her while they ate. He thought she
was not aware of his feelings, but she let him know
she was aware of what he had on his mind. And she
thought since he was a man of God, she didn't want
to stop or hinder what God had ordained for him to
do.

She wanted him to do what God would have him
to do. Although she knew how he felt about her, she
would continue to be his friend because if he would
leave his wife for her, then he would leave her for
someone else. And for that reason, they needed to
continue to pray and be good friends, so she could
help him through his crisis.

Chapter 10

All of a sudden, he realized he had been focusing on C.D. so much he didn't have the opportunity to focus on himself. For that reason, he was falling spiritually. He was attending churches, but he wasn't doing anything. He wasn't preaching. He wasn't doing that which he was ordained to do.

As a minister, if he read the Bible, it was just to prove a point. If he did something, it was because he was obligated. Therefore, he got in the lowest slump in his life. For the first time, he didn't even have the joy of saying, he knew the Lord. He was lower than before he met his wife because then he was a single man and was crying out for help. But now this time, it seemed as though he really didn't want help.

Because of him not wanting help, he could not go with C.D., who would continue to say, "Let's keep it as friends."

He was yearning to be with C.D.. He thought if he could find someone else to make C.D. jealous, then she would want him. He could then leave with C.D., who he really wanted to be with but was afraid.

Consequently, he met a young lady with the initials of L.W.. He told her about C.D.. Now in the meeting, L.W. said, "I want you to know I am not C.D., and if you come this way, you better be for real because I need a real man in my life."

Well, it was sad to say, he decided being with L.W. would help him get C.D. He found himself for the first time in an adulterous relationship. He thought it would be hurting and devastating to him, but he found out because he was so low, it only scratched the surface. All of a sudden the thing he thought would be so bad, he realized it wasn't so bad. Now, he needed C.D. to know about L.W.. And if he could get C.D. to find out about L.W., then maybe C.D. would come his way, and he could go that way with C. D..

Unfortunately, he did get involved with L.W., knowing he should stay away. He found himself committing adultery. He became so miserable, he wanted to confess to somebody about the situation. But he figured if he confessed, they would look at him as a nothing and a nobody. He thought being with L.W. was going to really produce the woman he needed in his life, not recognizing he was already married. So again, he thought he was going forward, but he found himself going backwards.

In the midst of going backwards in the relationship with L.W., his wife began to focus on C.D.. Finally, she decided to go to C.D.'s house to confront her.

His wife told C.D., "Well, I believe my husband is a man of God. I don't know what you did with my husband, but I will say this - that not only have you dealt with someone's husband, but you have also dealt with a man of God. And woe be unto you!"

C.D. called him and said she needed to leave him alone because his wife was trying to put a curse on her or trying to make something happen in her life. And since they were not sexually involved, she would appreciate it if he stayed away from her. He tried to convince C.D. the relationship needed to get better instead of end. But she pulled away.

So, now, he was more miserable. His wife called him when he was out of town and said she went to see his whore. Furthermore, she wanted him to get his clothes and get out. He knew he wasn't involved with C.D., so he wasn't worried. But he was thinking he was about to reap the benefits of his sexual experience with L.W..

L.W. was having problems with being married herself at the same time. As he talked more to L.W., he found she had never gone more than a year without having another person in her life. She said, "That's what makes her husband treat her right."

All of a sudden, a conviction come upon him that he left the bed and cried. He knew he couldn't continue the relationship with L.W. although he wanted attention from an individual. But L.W. was not about to give him the attention without the sexual encounter.

Well, he laid in the bed and talked to God. And in talking to God, he felt He wasn't listening. He became bitter at his wife.

His wife said she tried to talk to C.D., who had so much fear, she had a serious wreck right up from her house. Things began to happen. It really seemed like someway, somehow, God's wrath was about to come upon the preacher because it had already come upon C.D.. Nobody looked at L.W., who was doing all the spiritual damage. He tried to convince L.W. their relationship was not going to work because when he was with her, he was fine, but when he was alone, he felt bad.

Chapter 11

Shortly following the breakup with L.W., his wife decided she needed some attention. She met a mechanic, who she decided needed to work on her car. Of course, she wasn't getting any attention from her husband. She began to go after this guy or this guy began to go after her. Which way, he didn't know. Then she began to uphold this guy to his face. He, which had already put up with rejection from the beginning of their relationship when she conceived a baby, was determined he wasn't going to leave her. As he made it known, he would not leave her, she rubbed his face in what she was doing. He did know the mechanic was giving his wife money.

To investigate the situation, the preacher sent a young lady to the shop to talk to one of the guys over there. This guy told her about his wife. Come to find out, his wife was going with him. Not only was his wife going with the guy, but also they would sit and drink together.

They started out like she was supposed to be a sister, and he was supposed to be a deacon. But after a while, it changed from that. She said her husband was neglecting her, therefore, he needed to spend some time with her. She began to be there so much, even when her husband was in church service. Not only was she talking to the mechanic, but his wife was also talking to other guys because she began to go to clubs to meet other men. Her friend, who was jealous of her, told him about the other men.

Now, he was stressed out. He felt he was going right back to the thing he had said wouldn't happen again. He found himself the same way he was before he married his wife. He wished she would either get out of his life or straighten up and do right. Well, as fate would have it, while he looked at her, the devil took him down a downward trail.

L.W. thought being in an outside relationship was her way of keeping a happy home. As he prayed to come out of it, it seemed like God was not hearing him. Unfortunately, the messages he preached to teach people were just words. He didn't even have a desire to read the Bible anymore.

One day, L.W. said to him, "I didn't want to give

myself to my husband. I wanted to wait to be with you."

He thought this would be the death of him because her husband was beginning to get jealous of her, and she didn't care. And he thought, God if there was ever such a time he needed to be delivered, now was the time. So what he did was, he began to tell L.W., "That's okay."

At the time, C.D. decided to move out of town. He knew all hope was gone to ever get C.D. back into his life. She decided to let her mother and sister stay in her house while she moved back to her hometown.

He felt so bad because everything around him that represented righteousness was gone. He was at the end of the rope. He decided this was it. The best thing he could do was to get his clothes. Then he thought, if he got his clothes, then everybody would know. He didn't want everybody to know. So, he began to make a secret plan to be a missing person.

To remedy the situation, he made plans to move up North. Then as fate would have it, two weeks before he got ready to move, his wife took sick. As she took sick, he took her to the hospital. At the time, the doctor asked him, "How many children do you have?" He told him. Then the doctor said, "Do you have room for one more?"

He asked, "Why would you ask that?"

The doctor said, "Because she is going to have another baby."

At that time, he turned and said, "God, why?" Out of all the years he wanted to have a baby from her, he couldn't. But the very time when he made plans to go forward, now he found himself going backwards in having to deal with a baby.

Chapter 12

The news about his unfaithful wife made him cry out to God. He said, "God, I am not even worthy to call myself saved, let alone to call myself a preacher. I brought a reproach to Your name. I did all the things I should not have done. But even in that, Your mercy has kept me."

That was one of the lowest points in his life. He lost his house because he lost his job. He now was living in a government project. And he said, "Lord in the midst of all this, You have yet kept Your hands on me. Why? I don't know. But right now, I don't know anything."

As he said that, the Lord said, "You do know that you are saved. And you do know that I called you. And because I called you, you need to get yourself up and begin to move in that direction."

God had spared him from a lot of disgrace, a lot of pain and suffering that he could have experienced if people really knew what was going on. So, he began to make an about face. He began to move in a direction, with the help of God, to start all over again. And he made it up in his mind, even if nothing else, he was going to be saved himself. He was no longer going to allow his wife to drive him to someone else to give him peace and comfort. He realized God made him for a purpose. But as he began to move in the direction to go forward, his wife ridiculed him with condemnation. Some of it was because she was pregnant. Some of it was because she just didn't know how to deal with herself as well. But as God began to bless him, he began to go forward. God opened up his eyes and gave him a revelation on areas that were going on in his life, which so many people were experiencing, also.

God let him know he couldn't look to his wife, even though he loved her dearly, to be that woman for him. He looked to other women to get the relationship he desired, which made him feel he was someone special.

He began to look over his life at all he had done. It was like plowing through the sea. He only had waves to show for all the heartaches and pain, and the things that were accomplished. Now, as he looked in the direction God led him, a direction that would cause others to look at him as someone knowledgeable. Knowing he was illiterate when God called him and had gone through life as a rejected vessel. So, God took him into His Word and showed him why he thought when he was going forward, he was going backwards.

God said, "I called you. I ordained you before the foundation of the world. And because I made you a Black man, I made you to be the head and not the tail."

Many people often talk about being Black and proud. But until you have been a REAL Black man, blackest of the Black man, you can never experience the power of being Black. As he sought God's will and purpose, God took him back to Genesis. God showed him how He formed man from the dust of the earth. Anytime you want to grow the best plants or anything from the earth, you must use dark soil. He said, "God, I need more assurance."

God said, "You must realize I gave the Word of God to the Black man first. And because you are that inheritance, you should be able to go forth in it, greater and more powerful than any other. When you look at the children of Israel, they were the only ones who had the true and living God. But when you look in the Scriptures, you will see God led Jethro, Moses father-in-law, who was a high priest." Of course we all know Moses married an Ethiopian. That's why Miriam persecuted him because the woman he married was a darker complexion than they.

But, not only did God use Jethro to bring wisdom and knowledge, Jethro gave him a solution from God. Therefore, Jethro had to have the Word of God and had to be of God to instruct Moses, who was one of the greatest prophets in that time. It didn't stop there. God showed him how the Black man turned his back on God, who sought after the world and the things of the world. The more he sought after the things of this world, we became a heathenistic nation. We began to hate, devour and to kill one another. But God looked upon the Black race again and said, "I want to pull a people out of a people."

The time of slavery was just beginning to take the weaker vessels. Because the Bible teaches us in Corithians that God takes the things that are despised and rejected, the weaker things to bring to naught the things that are strong.

God took the weaker people, allowed them to be sold, and allowed them to go into bondage for 400 years. The purpose for them to go into bondage was

God had to change their outlook because they could no longer continue to serve the false, idol gods and go through the pagan customs and pagan rituals that they did in Africa. Therefore, God brought them to a strange land, which we call America. Most people looked at it as a tragedy, but God showed him it was a blessing because He was bringing him forth. He believed God brought us to this nation and changed our names. In the Bible, when Jacob sought God's face and wrestled with an angel, he came to the true knowledge of himself. The first thing God did was give him another name.

We have people in our society trying to reach back and find old names. Even young Blacks today are naming their children by names they say are from our heritage. But God wanted us to leave those names. He wanted us to leave that way of life because He wanted us to raise a nation up here.

On numerous occasions, He has shown that we were the head. When we look at the education programs, the teaching and discoveries, we find the Black man came in the forefront. When we look at medicine, doctors, the first heart transplant person and the great things of medicine, we find the Black man has risen to the top. When we look at sports, there is no question in our mind who is the leader - the Black man. When we look at entertainment, whether it is singing or dancing, again the Black man is on top. Yes, even when it comes to serving the Lord. No group of people know how to serve Him and cry out to Him like the Black man.

So, the young man, being a fifty-year-old Black man, looked back at the devastating things he brought forth on the name of Christ. That he brought an open shame by lying, stealing, committing adultery and breaking other commandments. But, God's mercy and His goodness allowed him to write this to let you know, you don't have to look for a new way out. You don't have to look for a different pathway. Even where you are now, God can bring forth deliverance. As a matter of fact, He wants to bring forth deliverance.

You see, you have no concept, no blueprint to make you how you are and what you are. But, you were made how God made you. You had nothing to do with how you were made, the time you came on this earth, and the lifestyle you choose to live. A lot of times, we believe we make our own choices. However, satanic forces or self-control or the devil's desire in pleasing the flesh controlled your choices when you were in sin.

Here's the problem. When we come over to Christ, the preachers make us feel and we believe everything we once did or had problems with are forgotten. The Scriptures say, "*If any man be in*

Christ Jesus, he is a new creature. Old things are passed away. Behold all things become new." By now, I know you realize the preacher in this story is me, Brother James Ware.

Chapter 13

All things become new as we grow in the Lord. There are things that the Lord will take away from you. He will give you the ability to walk away from such things as drugs and alcohol. The Scriptures say, *"We are born in sin and shaped in iniquity."* Whether you believe it or not, you carry your mother's or your father's sin once you come to Christ.

You say, "Wait a minute, Brother Ware, I don't see how you can say, I carry my mother's and my father's sin. Well, if you are honest with yourself, you will find some things they are doing and have done in the past, you have the same desires to do now. And the reason you have the same desires now is because you have inherited their sins.

Now, my mother was a woman of the world and loved the streets. When I came to Christ, I thought I wouldn't have that problem because I didn't love the streets, so to speak. However, at the same time, I had her nature to want somebody in my life to sooth me. And because I had this need to be soothed, I kept getting lonely women who were trying to satisfy their flesh. The fact I had a good job, I was able to be a blessing. All of them were not after money. A lot of them were after companionship.

We think by taking on an office as a minister or deacon, we are exempt from sin. That is a fantasy world. We all must deal with our problems. If we don't deal with them daily, the problems will get us down. As we deal with them daily, then we will find ourselves keeping our bodies. That's why Paul said, "*I must keep my body under subjection, lest I preach to others. I, myself, will become a castaway.*" A lot of good ministers have become a castaway simply because of the fact that they didn't have anyone to believe what was going on in their lives.

We see famous preachers who have failed because of women and money. We also see people of the Bible who failed because of women or money.

My wife had a very good friend who was jealous of her. Therefore, she made herself available to me. Now, she might have not meant to do it. She might have not said, well, I'm available, but she was always there. As time passed, I never confronted the friend. However, I always had in the back of my mind she always needed or wanted someone like myself in her life. And because she was my wife's friend, I never approached her in that way. The truth of the matter was, she believed I would confront my wife about it.

When my wife was going out, she would be the one to give me information, which would cause me to do better. God put ministers around me who had the same problems, but they were not able to deal with them. Each one of them left their wives. There were three of them. Each time, they said when they left their wives, they did better. I found out they were doing worse. They said they had gotten happiness and peace. They were saying it with their lips, but I saw they were in worse shape. So, that was a message to me.

Shortly after I began to see the message, then all of a sudden I reached the lowest point in my life with my finances. I did not have anything. Someone came into my life who seemed to be sincere at heart. If I could sit down and order a person from God, I would order that person. I believed she was genuine, but I kept reminiscing on what happened to the other preachers. Therefore, I didn't make that fatal leap or move forward in going into a relationship with her. A lot of times, you will see what you want, and the devil will set the stage. He doesn't make us do anything as I told you earlier.

He sets the stage, but he can't make you do any-thing. When the stage is set, you have a choice in Christ Jesus. You didn't have that choice before you came to the Lord. You did what was told or what your flesh desired. But once you came to Christ, basically what He said was, "*He that comes to Me. He that the Son sets free is free indeed.*" Meaning, I have freedom to leave the prison or stay in the prison. I have freedom not to commit adultery or to commit adultery. Because of my freedom, I choose how I take it, and what I do with it.

Most of the time, we find ourselves struggling in some areas of our lives. It may not be lust of the flesh. It may be in acquiring materialistic things. It may be trying to keep up with the world in style. And it may be just out right wanting to have your way. The truth of the matter is, this is what we do. We make these choices knowing He said, "*Seek those things from above and not things on this earth.*" The reason He is telling us to seek those things from above and not things on the earth is because He already knows the devil sets the stage. Satan can make your life miserable in Christ. This is what I am saying.

Chapter 14

In order to live the abundant life, do not seek after the desires of the flesh, which are strong in different areas. Even now that I am a man who has lived a half a century, I must still battle with my flesh. When the enemy works at one hand, he works at the other hand, too. He will cause the wife not to do the things she is supposed to do. Therefore, Satan will present someone who will make a proposition, who will love to do those things the man desires. That's where we have to make a stand. We have to take a stand and say, "OK, God has given me the ability."

Well, you say, "Brother Ware, now that you are in a relationship, you have what the Bible calls a concubine." The truth of the matter is, no I don't, but I could very easily have one. I choose not to because of the fact I am seeking to know what God has purposed for me. I have lived the majority of my believer's life trying to do it myself. No one is able to do anything. The Bible tells us, "It is not to him that willest, nor to her that runs, but God that shows mercy." So if it's not to him that willest, nor to her that runs, then it is in the Lord God. Therefore, He has already predestinated me to inherit the things he has for me. Now, the only thing I need to do is to continue to walk. Yes, the temptations will come. Yes, I am going to continue to meet the people. You know the sad thing is, we are mistaken that the older we get, the less the temptations will come. Until you are able to overcome temptation, it will continue to come. It is going to get worse and worse. And even at living half a century, it is just as bad as when I lived a quarter of a century.

Being twenty-five years old when temptation was presented to me, I wanted to dive into it because I thought it would bring me joy. After being into it, I realized the joy wasn't what I thought it was. But it was His mercy. It is not because of my goodness that I am still a minister of the gospel. It's not because of my goodness that I am yet proclaiming to be saved. I used to look at the people of the past, and I thought they had a spotless life. I look at the people in the church today, and I think they have a spotless life. But oh my brothers and sisters, as I began to get closer to these people, I began to see they have all dealt with problems. So what is the problem solver?

I believe Solomon said, "*Now let us hear the conclusion of the whole matter,*" in Ecclesiastes 12:13. He said, he had experienced these things. And in experiencing these things, he realized there was no joy. So, what am I saying? "Hear the conclusion of the whole matter. Fear God and keep His commandments. This is the whole duty of man."

We begin to delight ourselves in God. It doesn't matter what condition you are in if you understand that you know who you are. Understand God has you in this position to serve a purpose. Anything that is going on in your life is going on for a purpose. It is not able to happen except God permits it. He must allow Satan to tempt us. But He has told us in I Corinthians 10:13, *"He will not allow us to be tempted above that which we are able to bear."* Because He knows this, and He knows where we are. I'm telling some of you, who are in the position you are in, whether it is drugs, alcohol, lust of the flesh, or trying to get a bank account, it doesn't mean anything! If you can get these things, then you really don't have the love of Christ within you. Not only that, it doesn't mean anything if you accomplish these things because you are not going to be fulfilled. When I talk about the women, I had them, but it wasn't fulfilling. I didn't love them enough to step out and leave my wife. You know why? Because I realized they were not my fulfillment. They just had something that looked shiny, but wasn't fulfilling.

So, it is with those of you who are seeking after drugs. Saying you are going to get over this. I'm saying the only way you are going to overcome this is, you have to present your body as Romans 12:1&2 says, "*I beseech you therefore brethren by the mercy of God to present your bodies as a living sacrifice, holy and acceptable unto God.*" You have to put you on the altar. You have to say, "God I tried to quit. I couldn't do it. I had to face the fact, even to this day, God I have a lustful mind and a lustful spirit shaped in iniquity." I put me on that altar as a living sacrifice. And once I put me on the altar, then God always makes a way out even when I can't see a way out. So, when I am presented with something that looks good and sounds good that makes me feel like this will be the answer, this will be my deliverance, then I will sin on the other hand.

Those of you who want to be delivered or feel you can't be delivered, then I am here to tell you, understand God chose you. You were predestinated. And if you were predestinated to live that more abundant life, then it is a possibility you need to get back to the Bible teachings. I am not talking about denominational teaching. When we read the Bible with a denomination, we read it according to that which we believe. We need to seek out the will of God. When I was reading the Bible, I was saying, "God, David was a man after your own heart. If he could have other wives and concubines, then how is it so wrong? You said, You have no respect of person." Therefore, I had to say, "Wait a minute. I'm going through what I am going through because of a weak spot. I have to deal with that weak spot." If I don't deal with it daily, then it will be my downfall. Would it cause me to lose my salvation? I don't think so. I believe if you are truly born of God, you are born of God. And I don't think a particular sin will cause you to lose out. You do, however, pay a price for disobedience.

Now, here's the difference between the man who is born of God, and the man who is not born of God. The man who is born of God will rationalize things out, will seek out how to be delivered, and how to be set free. Well, on the other hand, the person that is not born of God will continue to justify and pretty soon they will begin to do whatever.

You say, Brother Ware, it seems to me, you are saying I cannot be delivered if I tried to. What Brother Ware is saying is, it is not you being delivered. You've got to understand. The only thing you can do is put you on the altar. Give you to the Lord. Cry out and say, "God, I have tried it, but I can't do it." Been there! Tried it! I have done the things I thought would bring forth my deliverance. But in trying it, no deliverance came. You must be real with God, real with yourself, and begin to come away from the denomination reading the Bible. I often tell people, start with your program of reading the Bible fifteen minutes in the morning and fifteen minutes at night. Give fifteen minutes of your time with just you and the Lord. And be honest with God.

The problem with people today is, we are not honest. The reason we are not honest because we have lied so long, and it feels so good being something we are not. We find ourselves liking that lie. But you must be honest because He already knows.

Chapter 15

God knew I had a desire for a particular type of woman. And since He knew it, the devil knew it, too. Therefore, the devil would put those types of individuals in my life. I understand, God made me this way for His glory regardless of what shortcomings I have. It is nothing but flesh. The real me loves God. The real you can love God. The only reason you can connect with the Lord and be a true connection is that you have to surrender you to Him. And when you surrender you to Him, then you will understand you are not a superhuman. Everybody has flaws. Everybody has shortcomings. The greatest preachers you know have shortcomings just like you. But the truth of the matter is, you are able to deal with your shortcomings. Romans the Twelfth Chapter has given us our deliverance and our way out.

Because of denominations, we feel going to church is the way. You can go to church on top of different churches, change this church, go to church on this particular time, go here and go there. You are not going to get delivered. You can have this person to pray for you and that person to pray for you while you wait on some type of quick fix. That's not going to happen. But what's going to happen if you remember Romans 12:1 & 2, "*I beseech you therefore brethren by the mercy of God that you present your body as a living sacrifice. Holy and acceptable unto God, which is your reasonable service.*"

So it's saying present your body to the Lord. Give it to God. Lord, I have a problem with these things. Whatever you're going through, present it to Him. And once you present it to Him, then, the next verse says, "*Be not conformed to this world but be ye transformed by the renewing of your mind.*" Begin to renew your mind. How do you renew your mind? As I told you, by reading your Bible fifteen minutes in the morning, fifteen minutes in the evening and spending fifteen minutes of uninterrupted time with God. In doing so, God can begin to transform your mind. As you renew your mind, then you may be able to prove that which is good and acceptable, perfect will of God. Will you stop going through your struggling? No, you will not because you are in the flesh. And the Bible says, sin was condemned in the flesh. But will you be able to overcome it? Yes, you will. Why? Because you presented it to the Lord. You put it on the altar to God.

I truly pray that those of you before you make a decision, try doing this. Then will you see, for your whole life you were going forward, but you were walking backwards, closer to the Lord. As a baby, you lived to be a certain age. And as an adult, when you became a certain age, you realized you were coming closer to the end of your life. I am closer to the end of my life now than at the beginning. But at the same time, I was able to overcome certain areas of my life. I realize I have to put it on the altar and present it to God.

I pray this book will change your life and understand He truly wants you to live this life more abundantly. Regardless of your situation, if you are in a shack, in an apartment or even if you have a house on the hill, it doesn't matter unless you have a true connection to that which He will have you to do.

May Heaven smile upon you. And may God make you be that vessel He has called and chosen you to be because we are going forward, but we are walking backward.

God Bless you.

ABOUT THE AUTHOR

James S. Ware was born in Abbeville, South Carolina, on December 15, 1952, to James and Sally Weir. He is the father of five children and is a devoted husband to his lovely wife of twenty-five years, E. Ann Ware.

Brother Ware, as he likes to be called, received Jesus in his life as his Lord and Saviour in March 1976. After receiving Christ, he knew he had a calling to minister the Word. He accepted his calling in September 1976 at New Life in Christ Baptist Church under Pastor Walter Jones. Four years later, he was ordained as a minister of the Gospel of Christ under Pastor L. H. Commons of Lighthouse Tabernacle of East Point, Georgia.

In March 1984, he became the Pastor and Founder of The Holy Temple of the Lord's Church, where he now presides. For over thirteen years, he served in prison ministries in Dekalb and Fulton Counties as well as the chaplain of the Divergence Center in the Atlanta Metropolitan area.

The Lord has given Brother Ware a burden for the souls of men. Therefore, he started a ministry,

Believers Walking in the Way of Righteousness. He feels he has the solution to the problems people are trying to find. That is, to come back to the Bible and believe in it. He feels people are in the position he was in for many years, running to and fro, not being able to do anything and calling themselves being "in the will of God." The truth of the matter is, people are out of His will, yet proclaiming to know His will. The Bible says, "*There is a way that seems right to a man, but the end thereof is the way of death.*" Proverbs 14:12

Some people's definition of a Christian is "one who believes," but the true definition of a Christian is one who professes belief in Jesus Christ and follows His ways.

To find out more about Brother Ware, Believers Walking in the Way of Righteousness and his radio broadcast, please visit his website at: www.brotherware.org.

His mailing address is: P.O. Box 161001
Atlanta, Georgia
30321
Fax: 404-361-5592

The Literary Connection

This book was prepared and edited by Deeva Denez of The Literary Connection. If you need your manuscript typed, edited, and published, please contact The Literary Connection at 2794 Stardust Ct., Decatur, Georgia 30034. You may also email her at deeva_denez@yahoo.com or visit her website at www.geocities.com/deeva_denez.